PARTNERING ASSISTING CARING ENDING

PACE
toward peace

What Everyone
Should Know About
End-of-Life Care

KIM GLADSTONE, RN, CHPN
LAURIE WOLF, PhD

PACE Toward Peace
What Everyone Should Know About End-of-Life Care
Kim Gladstone, RN, CHPN and Laurie Wolf, PhD
A Happy Daisy, LLC

Published by A Happy Daisy, LLC, St. Louis, MO
Copyright ©2020 Kim Gladstone, RN, CHPN and Laurie Wolf, PhD
All rights reserved.

Cover and Interior design: Davis Creative, DavisCreative.com

Library of Congress Cataloging-in-Publication Data

Library of Congress Control Number: 2020908150

Kim Gladstone, RN, CHPN and Laurie Wolf, PhD

PACE Toward Peace: What Everyone Should Know About End-of-Life Care

ISBN: 978-1-7343216-0-9

Library of Congress subject headings:

    1. SEL010000 SELF-HELP / Death, Grief, Bereavement   2. FAM014000 FAMILY & RELATIONSHIPS / Death, Grief, Bereavement   3. MED041000 MEDICAL / Hospice Care see Terminal Care

    2020

ATTENTION CORPORATIONS, UNIVERSITIES, COLLEGES AND PROFESSIONAL ORGANIZATIONS: Quantity discounts are available on bulk purchases of this book for educational, gift purposes, or as premiums for increasing magazine subscriptions or renewals. Special books or book excerpts can also be created to fit specific needs. For information, please contact A Happy Daisy, LLC, daisy.ldw@gmail.com.

This book is dedicated to our Moms:

Evelyn Lucile Zysset Wolf (Dillie) and
Mary Ann Fuchs Prives.

They taught us about life
when we were young,
aging while we grew old,
and end-of-life as they neared theirs.

Thank you.

Table of Contents

Introduction

Mae has lived with cancer for nearly 30 years. She is a clever, accomplished wife, mother, writer, artist, and disrupter. She lives every day with the knowledge that death is coming and because of that, she lives large. She's also superstitious and won't say the words "death" or "cancer" out loud. Now in her mid-70s, she still expects to live twenty more years, and she's lightening up just a bit on her superstitions. At a recent holiday dinner, she joked with her family that when her time comes, she wants to be made into soup. Her family members were astonished, aghast, and grossed out. They protested loudly until one niece spoke up, offering several recipes that could be Mae's soup. One would be spicy, another sweet, and of course, one a little sour. No one was grossed out anymore, and no one will ever forget that lead-in or the discussion that followed.

Mae's creativity and ability to talk about her mortality in a creative way gives us a blueprint to change how we look at death. Mae and her family may be facing mortality, but they've chosen to do it consciously with love and laughter—a guaranteed recipe for an experience of a lifetime.

This book is dedicated to those who dare to think about the last six months of life so they can live every moment, in the moment.

Why this book now?

Public health advances, improved technology, and medicine have evolved to lengthen our lifespans. Many people now live well into their 80s and 90s, and unlike people who lived a century ago, most of us won't die quickly—within hours or days that is. Most of us will die gradually, over several months, from a chronic disease that we've lived with for months, years, or even decades. For the most part, we can't predict exactly when the last breath will be, but it's becoming more common that we can predict when it's coming.

Even though this change is occurring and we now have a better idea about when and what we might die from, we haven't quite caught up with what it means for each of us and what could be done to improve the experience of dying gradually.

What you should know:

- When a life-limiting diagnosis becomes known, a ripple effect occurs. The dying person is clearly the most profoundly impacted; but their caregiver, their family, and their friends are impacted too. Death happens to an individual, but dying is typically a communal experience. This book describes the impact and actions that can be taken by the different people involved in a gradual death.
- This book is not for everyone. Our cultural and societal views on death influence how we experience the death of our loved ones, as well as our own death. This resource is for those who are curious, or are planners, or those who want to help but don't know how. It is for those who want to know more about the process of gradual death, or those who want to die in a way that keeps their family and friends involved and healthy. Many people have the instinct to do what is helpful in any situation including dying, but many more could benefit by learning more about

what's happening and by thinking through how they want to participate.

- Reading this book may make some people more or less anxious about what's ahead. If it increases anxiety, we recommend talking to a medical professional with experience in end-of-life care, ideally someone who is knowledgeable about hospice care. They are well aware of the dying process and what comes with it. Those who work in hospice are expert at providing both information and compassion. If you choose hospice care, experts are there for you throughout the process. Take advantage of that expertise. If hospice is not an option, talk to a healthcare professional who is comfortable talking about end-of-life care.

- This book is purposefully short to make it a fast read. There are plenty of resources about end-of-life care to learn more about a specific aspect or disease. This book provides an overview of the process with key information presented all in one place. It can be read repeatedly at different phases of the dying experience, for example, when someone you love receives a life-limiting diagnosis and again as they go through each phase.

- There is no way to predict when people will die. There is, however, a general rule that provides some guidance: if functional changes (a decline in ability to do what a person could do before) are happening month to month, then the dying person will likely have months to live. If changes are happening week to week, then they will have weeks to live, and if changes are happening day to day, then they will have days to live. This book provides information about the changes that occur as those months, weeks, and days progress. It provides shared terminology for the dying person, and their caregiver(s), family, and friends to communicate effectively.

- This book is not a recipe. Timelines are only estimates. By definition, hospice care covers the last six months of life so this common time frame provides a standard to which we can note the similarity or dissimilarity between expected deaths. During this time, there are recognizable patterns that apply to many deaths. At the same time, it's important to remember everyone dies differently. As you and your family go through this process, you may very well observe your experience is not what is noted here. Hopefully, though, the book will provide you something to compare your experience to and will offer helpful hints along the way.

- Every family has its level of function and dysfunction. When a family member dies, the function and dysfunction in the family can escalate, decrease, or both, at different times in the process. This pattern is normal. The end of a life is one of the most significant experiences of our lives, so it's no surprise individuals react differently to each phase. It is the intention that this book promotes communication and peace—but it's useful to know ahead of time that it may not.

- This book is not a medical book. Medical professionals receive education and training on many of the issues shared in this book. They should be your resource for specific questions.

- Pace yourself and others. Hopefully, this book is a helpful resource for you. Understand that although it may help you to know the information in this book, it may not be the right time for others to hear it. Hospice professionals routinely share information with the patient and family only when they appear ready and to need it. The goal is to not overwhelm them. This practice of sharing what is helpful at the right time may assist you in avoiding unnecessary suffering. Before you share what you've learned from this book, consider if sharing it will help or hurt. Is the other person ready to hear it? One way to determine their readiness is to offer a small amount of information, for example, "I found a book that talks about the phases people go through at the end of their lives. It's for both the dying person and the people who love them." If they don't ask you more about it, they probably aren't ready to hear about it. Use the same technique with other aspects of this book; introduce the topic and see if they ask for more. Be prepared to find that they may never be ready.

- Information in this book is divided into roles: dying person, caregiver, and family. We recommend that you read all the sections including the Appendices, regardless of your role. We placed the information where we thought it fit best, but people may find each section useful even though it's not the role they have. Roles can change, too. Family members may become primary caregivers as death approaches. The dying person may also want to make different decisions once they know more about what their family may experience.

- This book is intended to help people think and talk about how we die today. The more we explore and consider how we die, the more we can learn how to decrease the suffering of the dying person and those around them and even take advantage of the opportunities an expected death brings.

Perspectives

In this book we offer a shared vocabulary about what is experienced from the perspective of the dying person, the caregiver, and the family. In addition, we address the environment and how it can be modified to support the dying person, the caregiver, and the family.

Most importantly, we introduce a model to differentiate four phases people go through when dying gradually. PACE is a way to share a vocabulary or way of thinking about what is occurring and what is experienced by each person in each phase, based on the role they play. Knowing what to expect for yourself and others provides opportunity to prepare, support, and experience each phase fully. Here are the four phases of a gradual death:

P = PARTNERING: This phase is similar to many partnerships, where two people work equally but with different specialties, sharing in most decisions and work. (CHAPTER 1)

A = ASSISTING: This phase is when the dying person allows or asks the caregiver to make decisions and needs assistance with daily activities. (CHAPTER 2)

C = CARING: This phase is when the caregiver makes all decisions and is responsible for all daily activities. (CHAPTER 3)

E = ENDING: In this phase, as the dying person disengages with this world, the caregiver remains in the decision-making role and is responsible for all decisions and work. (CHAPTER 4)

Appendix A (PACE Mnemonic) provides a quick reference that combines the perspectives of each of the phases. Chapters 1 through 4 covers each part of the model described above.

Here's how we talk about each person in the PACE Model to show their perspective:

Dying Person – After several discussions, we settled on this simple and to-the-point description. We thought it might also be helpful to some people to hear these words repeated, that is, after they get over the initial shock of how the words sound, so the concept of dying becomes more normalized.

Caregiver(s) – Primary caregiving usually falls to one person, but it could be more than one person. For example, at some point in the process, an adult child could join a parent in caring for the other parent.

Family – The definition of family is broad and includes the people who know they are family, not just blood relatives.

Environment – The place where the dying person lives during each phase.

The medical field is working on shared vocabulary too. Palliative care focuses on symptom control and the patient's goals or quality of life. It can be provided even when a curative treatment is occurring. Hospice care is a kind of palliative care that is offered when a person is not expected to live more than six months. The focus of hospice care is on comfort care.

Hospice Explained

A hospice team is composed of a doctor, nurse, social worker, chaplain, and volunteers. Many hospice teams include other professionals such as massage, music, or art therapists. They all provide care, comfort, and guidance to the dying person and importantly, to their family as well.

In the United States and many other countries, hospice is now a well-established, well-defined, and relatively well-enough funded service to provide support to people during the last six months of life. Resources involved in hospice care lean toward patient-focused care, and they eliminate or minimize invasive and machine-driven care.

Hospice care is not, as many people believe, a death sentence. Whatever disease process is involved— and not the receipt of hospice care—is what will cause death. Hospice care does not hasten death. Studies show those that those on hospice experience less pain and trauma and live as long or even longer than those who do not receive hospice care because hospice care focuses on the patient's daily needs, not on aggressive treatments that can have serious, and sometimes deadly, side effects.

Qualification for hospice depends upon the particular disease process and includes both objective measures and physician judgment. If you have questions about whether you or your loved one qualifies for hospice, talk to your doctor or contact a hospice provider. Ask for a hospice assessment. And here is the best news: Medicare and most health insurance plans now cover hospice care.

It's important to understand the role of hospice. If hospice occurs in the home, the caregiver and family remain the primary support for the dying person. The caregiver is responsible for delivering most of the care related to daily activities—directly or through contracting with a private duty company to provide that care. The role of hospice is to provide medical expertise, direct treatment (e.g., wound care or placement of a catheter), treatment plans, and medication, along with emotional and spiritual support during the death, and bereavement process. Hospice is not responsible for dressing, feeding, assisting the dying person to the toilet, or moving them from bed to a chair. Hospices usually offer help with bathing two times a week, but for the most part, members of the hospice team provide direction on how best to do daily activities. They are not responsible for direct care 24 hours a day. What they do is join the dying person, caregiver, and family on the journey and share their expert and invaluable knowledge with each new phase.

Hospice can also take place in a hospice house or nursing home, or in specially designated beds in a hospital. Payment for this 24-hour care depends on many things. A medical social worker is the best resource for understanding what will work for any particular situation.

There is a growing movement to have daily care in the home routinely covered by hospice. For many people, particularly those without a lot of resources, this change could improve their end-of-life experience dramatically. For now, even without daily care provided, hospice is an extraordinary support for the dying person and their family. Hospice nurses and doctors provide medical care and support. Hospice social workers provide information and guidance for financial, legal, or situational issues. Hospice chaplains offer a resource to bring comfort or to complement a dying person's spiritual practice.

Hospice routinely provides medications for comfort. These are medications that relieve pain, shortness of breath, constipation, nausea, or anxiety, or anything related to the diagnosis that qualified the dying person for hospice. It supplies pads for the bed, diapers, wipes, mouth care, wound care, and catheters. It also covers DME (durable medical equipment), which includes things like a hospital bed, over-the-bed table, walker, wheelchair, oxygen and suction machines, shower chair, and bedside commode.

Unfortunately, many people don't consider hospice until the last days or weeks of life. But hospice care doesn't work as well if it only happens for a week or less. It takes time to meet with the hospice team, to get to know one another, and for the hospice team to learn how best to support the dying person and their family.

Hospice is the care that provides patients and their families with the most helpful support for a deeply personal and communal experience. Those who delay or avoid hospice miss one of the best parts of modern healthcare.

Ideally, we all should talk with our doctors well in advance of the end of life (e.g., with our primary care doctor at yearly physicals, and with our medical specialist once a life-limiting diagnosis occurs), to communicate what kind of care we desire when death is inevitable.

PACE Toward Peace

The working title of this book was "A PACE to Live and Die By," but a dear friend who is a poet, and writer pointed out that we left out one of the most important experiences that occurs when people face death. He noted that when a person's life is coming to an end, it is their essence that comes forth.

He was right! We added a section for ESSENCE and changed the title to PACE Toward Peace.

Chapter 1

Partnering

Four phases occur when a person dies gradually. These phases occur regardless of us being conscious of them.

PARTNERING is the first phase. It's similar to many marriages, where two people work equally but with different specialties. They share in most decisions and daily activities (e.g., shopping, cooking, paying bills, and planning activities).

The partnering phase can seem like all is normal at times. Yes, there is a diagnosis that indicates death will occur within months. Still, there are times when this fact is not front of mind. The truth is known, but the effects aren't felt as they will be later. This phase gives a great gift of time to address outstanding issues with the motivation that comes from knowing there will not be time to address them later.

The Dying Person

During this phase, the dying person will likely be grieving. In 1969, Elisabeth Kübler-Ross gave us a vocabulary to share around the stages of grief. Now often referred to as categories because they don't necessarily happen in order, they are the benchmark to which others have compared and evolved our understanding of grief. The categories or stages of grieving offer a glimpse into how we as humans, process something as profound as death. Emotions will vary, but knowing our emotions are normal can provide some comfort. During this phase, emotions will come and go, resulting in the dying person being clear-thinking one moment and distracted the next.

Elisabeth Kübler-Ross's Stages of Grief

- Denial
- Anger
- Bargaining
- Depression
- Acceptance

Completing Important Tasks

The dying person may be worried about making sure everything is taken care of and may be overwhelmed by where to begin. Now is the time to make a list and complete those tasks that require attention, whether they are financial, legal, funeral details, or in mending relationships. Addressing priorities now will save a loved one additional work, money, and angst later. See Appendix B (Examples of Important Tasks).

Changes and Emotions in Partnering Phase

- Avoidance
- Confusion
- Fear
- Numbness
- Blame
- Frustration
- Anxiety
- Irritation
- Embarrassment
- Shame

- Feeling over-whelmed
- Lack of energy
- Helplessness
- Increasing desire to tell one's story
- Struggle to find meaning in what's happening
- New patterns
- Lack of control

Of course, some people will find the work of getting their affairs in order challenging. They may be in denial or feel overwhelmed with emotions. It may be complicated! If that's the case, now is the time to reach out for assistance. The hospice team is the right place to start. There are also social workers in private practice who specialize in preparation for end of life. Clergy can be helpful. Eldercare attorneys who specialize in end-of-life issues are also a useful resource. Some of this guidance and advice may cost money, but many are reasonably priced and it can be worth it to resolve issues now, avoiding more significant expenses later. Appendix B (Examples of Important Tasks), is a starting point for discussion with professional advisors.

Completing Personal Goals

Priorities will soon change toward daily needs, so it's time to take care of any unfinished plans for fun. Take that trip. Call your old friend. Be with family. Have a party. Go for a hike. Write that letter. Make a video or recording.

A "bucket list" is one way to involve others and create happy moments and memories. Do not put these plans off! The opportunity may arise again to do them later, but there is a risk it won't be as enjoyable as the disease progresses.

People who are introverted or who have spent their lives taking care of others may be less likely to ask for support in making their desires known. Resist this inclination. Your requests can be a gift to your loved ones. It will be comforting to others to know they gave you joy during a difficult time. Do it for them. The hospice team can help with this conversation and in making wishes come true.

In the Partnering phase, the decision-making process is likely to be similar to what has occurred in the recent past. Partners who have shared the load of life's work will continue to do so. But don't be lulled into established patterns. It's important to make plans for handing over responsibilities and decisions to a trusted, informed person.

In the Partnering phase, the dying person's physical ability will be near baseline (whatever the norm has recently been), but reaction time may be slower than usual because of medications or distraction.

Medications

Medications should be reviewed routinely with your medical team with comfort being the primary goal. When a person is dying, three approaches to medication change:
1. Medications taken for long-term goals should be stopped (e.g., cholesterol-lowering medications). Side effects increase as body systems slow, and there is no long-term

benefit to taking them. Work with your medical provider on this.

2. Relieving pain is the goal, without the usual fear of addiction. When pain medications don't work or stop working effectively, inform the hospice team so medication can be adjusted accordingly.

3. Every time pain medications are adjusted, medications that promote bowel regularity should be adjusted too. Some pain medications cause constipation.

Communicating

Now is the time to tell others what you want for the last days of your life. Being able to communicate wishes and share what brings joy will provide family and friends with information to show their love for you. A word of caution regarding getting too detailed about what wishes you share: well-meaning people may take them literally and when circumstances change—and they will—loved ones may think they are disappointing you because they could not precisely fulfill your wishes.

Guidelines for Communicating Your Preferences

End-of-life experiences are unpredictable. It's best to provide people with guidelines instead of mandates. Here are examples that allow for flexibility:

- "I would like music from the sixties and seventies played at some time during each day. My favorite artists are _____."
- "I want to be surrounded by family, but it doesn't have to be 24 hours a day with everyone. I just want to be able to say goodbye to everyone and know they are supporting me."
- "I am afraid of being alone, so do your best to make sure there is someone by my side or nearby at the end."
- "I'm an introvert. Give me time alone each day. I need to know you're near but not necessarily to have you in the room with me."
- "I prefer natural remedies, but reducing pain is my priority."
- "Having a clear head is my priority. I'm okay with pain."

If you mean it, it may be helpful to end the conversation with something like, "I know we can't predict what will happen, so when you have to make decisions, know that I appreciate, support, and love you, and I will not be upset or disappointed if plans change."

If there is something very important to you, however, now is the time to express what you absolutely don't want.

> "I do not want to be in pain."

> "I do not want to die in a hospital."

> "I do not want visitors except for close family, when I'm unconscious."

Transformation and Resilience

If the dying person is concerned about how loved ones will do emotionally after their death, they can take comfort in recent evidence that the death of a loved one can be transformational for many people. It's true that the people you love and who love you will never be the same after your death. They may struggle, and it will be difficult for them, but your presence in their lives and them learning to cope without your physical presence also provides them with an opportunity to grow. Of course, your death is not what anyone would choose to create transformation, but it can help to know that we humans are built to be resilient. You can encourage this perspective in how you speak with your loved ones or in writings, videos, or gifts you choose to give them before or after your death.

The Caregiver

The caregiver will likely be going through some of the same emotional ups and downs as the dying person. It can be helpful to use language to label "grieving" as what we do internally and "mourning" as the outward expression of grief. Both are essential. Mourning, however, is critical for the caregiver. Mourning promotes a healthier approach to a life-changing loss. Defining mourning with personal statements can help identify this necessary and helpful coping process.

Mourning Statements

"My outward expression of grief occurs when I talk with my dying loved one, friends, and family about what's going on and when I seek out support about our thoughts and needs."

"I don't usually cry, but when I cry now, it shows how much this person means to me. I may not like it, but crying is a natural way to express grief and mourn."

Circles of Support

Now is a good time for the caregiver to identify the people they will communicate with and lean on for help in the coming months. Picture circles of support with the dying person's closest family and friends in the center. This center circle includes the people you'll call when death occurs. They are the people likely to stay in touch during all phases. It's also helpful to understand that even if they are available to support the caregiver, they will need support themselves as well. Therefore, they may or may not always be able to provide all the support needed for the dying person or caregiver.

Circles of Support

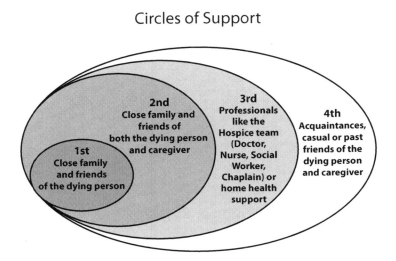

The second circle includes people who are also close to the caregiver. This group is the most likely to be available to support the caregiver. Examples include faith communities, social groups, or neighbors. When these people ask what they can do, it will pay off to have specific tasks in mind.

It may be helpful to ask:

"Can you call me in a month and ask again?"

"Would you bring us a dinner one night next week?"

"Can you help with laundry?"

"Will you sit with (the dying person) while I run an errand?"

"Could you help with a phone chain or social media to keep people informed?"

"Can you create a schedule for people to help out as we get closer to their death?"

We give people a great gift when we accept and guide their offers to help. They get to demonstrate their love for both the dying person and caregiver. In turn, both the dying person and caregiver feel love and gain practical, needed support—not a freezer full of food they won't eat.

The third circle includes professionals, like the hospice team. The hospice team is new to most people and is often the most valuable resource for support for the dying person, the caregiver, and the family. It will pay off to explore the support available from the hospice team at every PACE phase, including bereavement support for the family after the death. This third circle also includes any outside providers who help with bathing, dressing, and other daily activities.

The fourth or outside circle includes people who are not as close to the dying person or caregiver. They are often excluded from the process but can be a valuable source of support. They may include friends from the past, students or co-workers, faith communities, letter carriers, grocery clerks, hairdressers, a doctor's office staff member—anyone with whom the dying person formerly socialized with, in a friendly manner. Support from this group is likely to come in the form of prayers and cards, and occasionally they will provide an unexpected source of joy. People in this outer circle may know the caregiver but not the dying person. Their support of the caregiver can offer a break to get away for a bit or to talk about their growing responsibilities, or to share a hug or knowing smile.

Email, texting, and social media apps provide a modern way to communicate with all the circles of support. If this interests you, reach out to your tech-savvy friends or family for help.

Self-care

The Partnering phase is the time for the caregiver to create a self-care plan. The "Eight Dimensions of Wellness" provide a comprehensive checklist for the caregiver to visit through each phase and then to share identified needs with their circles of support.

Examples of The Eight Dimensions of Wellness:

1. Physical – Am I able to get enough exercise? Am I eating healthy foods? Am I getting enough sleep?
2. Occupational – How will I manage daily work with caregiving during this and the next phases?
3. Intellectual – How will I access resources during this and the next phase?
4. Financial – What financial or legal issues do I need to understand and address?
5. Social – What am I doing to stay in touch with people and to avoid isolation?
6. Environmental – Is our environment pleasant and stimulating to support our well-being?

7. Spiritual – Where do I get my spiritual support? Is it time to reconnect with my faith?
8. Emotional – Who can (and can't) support my emotional needs at this point? Are we talking about what's happening, or are we keeping it inside?

If there are gaps or unanswered questions, mention these to the hospice team, medical professionals, or faith leader. They have the expertise to guide you.

The Family

If family is out of town, they should visit during this phase if possible. Family members may also come when death is closer, but now will be when the dying person can spend time with and enjoy their company.

A Critical Role: The Caregiver's Caregiver

If family is able, they should consider becoming the caregiver's caregiver. The role does not have to be formal or time-consuming. It may be only once or twice that this support is needed. Or they may become a daily or weekly source of support. Just make it a point to look for opportunities to support the caregiver.

The Caregiver Needs Support, Not Advice

Support also takes the form of providing the caregiver with confidence in their decisions and in letting them know you are aware of their role and appreciate it. This point cannot be overstated. Supporting the caregiver in their choices is a gift everyone involved can give. Giving this type of support is most natural for those who have been in the caregiver role in the past. They know that appreciative, encouraging words matter.

The Environment

It's time to assess your environment and make decisions. Where does the dying person want to be spending time now and as death approaches? Note that they may not be the same.

Does the dying person want to die at home? Is that possible? Although home is the option most people answer when surveyed, options are growing. You may decide that to spend time at an adult child's or friend's home, a hospice house, or a nursing home is the best option. You may want to be at home until near death, and then want to be moved to a hospice house. You may want to spend some time at a vacation home or in the country. What physical location makes sense for the dying person, caregiver, and family? Regardless of which is preferred or needed, now is the time to make and communicate your desires.

Consider changes to your environment. Safety for both the dying person and caregiver matters. There are several fundamental questions to ask as you imagine going through your days.

- How can we reduce the risk of falls?
- Who will lift you if you fall?
- How will the caregiver safely assist and move the dying person in the future without risk of injury to either?

Is the toilet, bath, or shower set up in a way that will allow for assistance when it's needed?

What do we need to learn about now to be prepared for later? (Hint: You need to learn about pressure ulcers, medication management, and hospice.)

What equipment will help?

Your hospice team can help with environmental concerns and questions.

Partnering Phase Final Thought

The Partnering phase provides time and energy to prepare for the next phases. Completing outstanding work during this phase helps to create the potential for a peaceful experience in the Assisting, Caring, and Ending phases.

For a quick reference outlining this phase go to Appendix C (PACE Checklist).

Chapter 2

Assisting

ASSISTING is the phase when the dying person allows or asks the caregiver to make decisions and needs assistance with daily activities (e.g., walking, dressing, cooking, bathing).

In the previous phase of Partnering, there are many times when life seems like normal. During the Assisting phase, changes are more apparent. Still, there is no one specific moment when the transition happens. It's evident, with a look back, that a new phase had begun. There will be a time, though, when it becomes clear that you are in the Assisting phase.

The Dying Person

There will be a loss of independence in the Assisting phase. Losing independence can be difficult for some people, especially those who highly value it. Frustration will likely occur, and dignity can be at risk.

As more of us experience a death that occurs gradually, there is fortunately growing research on how to maintain dignity throughout the process. Dr. Harvey Chochinov, Distinguished Professor of Psychiatry at the University of Manitoba, and his team developed a Dignity Model to teach the value of making dignity a conscious goal of health care. The model has many levels and provides a simple blueprint of three dignity-conserving practices for all of us: living in the moment, maintaining normalcy, and seeking spiritual comfort. When in doubt, work on these.

Dignity-Conserving Practices

- Living in the moment = not worrying about the future or past
- Maintaining normalcy = keeping a normal routine
- Seeking spiritual comfort = finding comfort within religious or spiritual beliefs

---

What Matters?

At first thought, what matters may be your appearance. But it may also be helpful to understand that what you look like, or what you need help with, is less important to your caregivers and family than your physical and mental well-being.

Right Now Matters

"Right now" is what we have. To bring yourself into the present moment, pay attention to your breath, or your feet on the floor, or where the bed or chair is touching your skin. Practice this several times a day or when you find your thoughts dwelling in the past or anxiously wondering about the future.

Routines Matter

Daily routines may be different than a year or six months ago, but there are some that can and should continue on, e.g., the morning newspaper, a cup of tea, or a favorite TV show. Prioritize them and communicate their importance.

Spirituality Matters

If you haven't already done so, consider if it will help to address spiritual needs at this point in the process.

The hospice team can help with this if there is not an existing connection to a spiritual advisor.

It's interesting to know that about 50 percent of people who identify as religious don't practice their faith. Even so, about 50 percent of those who aren't actively practicing turn back to their faith at the end of life. Chaplains trained in hospice care are experts at supporting and assisting as people come to terms with their spiritual selves. They are open to any version of religion, faith, or spirituality, meeting you where you are today, even if that means you're uncertain. Take comfort in the fact that you cannot surprise them. They've seen and heard everything. They do not judge. Their job is to help, and they often recount how much they learn from the people with whom they work. If a particular chaplain is not a good fit, mention it to them or another member of the hospice team. It is not the time to be politically correct. Tell them the type of person or chaplain that you would be comfortable having a candid conversation with. It will pay off to work with someone who meets your needs best. That said, the people who choose to devote their life to hospice chaplaincy are generally supportive for everyone.

Fall Hazards at Home

- Throw rugs
- Cords in walkways (oxygen tubes)
- Pets underfoot
- Clutter on floor or steps
- Raised or loose thresholds in doorways
- Unstable chairs
- Uneven surfaces
- Low toilet seats
- Lighting (too dark or too bright)
- Showers without chairs or grab bars
- Medications

As you need more energy to get through the day, the outside world may become less important. Social norms may also not be as relevant as they once were. This can be freeing.

In the Assisting phase, physical dependency is increasing. Reaction time is decreasing. If you were driving, you'll stop during this phase. Slower reactions also increase the risk of falling and the chance of being hurt from that fall. For example, a slower reaction time can mean there is not enough time during a fall to react with arms to protect your face or head. Face-plant injuries are common. Changes in the environment can help reduce the risk of falls. Look at your environment and eliminate fall hazards, if possible. See sidebar for a list.

Both the dying person and the caregiver can communicate with healthcare professionals using the term Activities of Daily Living or ADLs. ADLs is a nursing term that defines a set of activities necessary for daily self-care. The specific activities monitored and addressed by medical personnel are:

- Moving around (locomotion), walking
- Transferring or moving from one place to another
- Bathing
- Dressing
- Eating or feeding
- Personal hygiene
- Toileting

During the Assisting phase, you will need help with some or all of these activities to get through your day.

See Appendix D (Activities of Daily Living [ADLs]) for a more in-depth explanation.

Along with changes in daily activities, each disease process brings its own set of issues. People with cancer have problems that are different from people with heart disease or a neurological disease. Shortness of breath, trouble swallowing, swelling and pain are examples, and everyone is different. Your hospice team can provide guidance on specific issues that come up.

Energy reserves are decreasing, so it is likely there will be good and bad days. Improve the chance for prioritized activities or tasks to be accomplished by moving them to the day after a good rest. Provide a day for rest after a busy day.

Pain Meds and Constipation

It's important to adjust medications with the goal of comfort. Be aware that many pain meds cause constipation, so any time opioid pain medications are started or increased, liquid intake, medications, and food that promote regularity should be started or increased.

Opioid pain medications cause constipation, so any time they are started or increased, medications that promote regularity should be started or increased.

To avoid constipation:

- Do what you already know keeps you having a BM regularly.
- Start using a stool softener or laxative (e.g., MiraLAX®, Senna S,) when an opioid is started. A laxative (moves the bowel muscle) and stool softener (makes stool less hard). Both assist the colon in resuming normal movement of the intestines. The goal is to keep the stool soft and to stimulate the colon. Both "moosh and push" keeps a person on opioids regular.
- Increase laxatives and stool softeners as opioid dosages are increased.
- Increase fluid intake.
- Work with your medical provider if you aren't sure about any of the above.

The Caregiver

It is during the Assisting phase when the reality of the caregiver role sets in. It can be strange for everyone as roles change, and an adjustment period is typical. Being aware of this will help everyone cope with the changes.

The Assisting phase brings an increased daily workload for the caregiver as the dying person is more reliant on them. At the same time, the dying person's role is changing dramatically too. As they lose their independence, the caregiver can play a significant role in helping them maintain dignity.

The caregiver can focus on dignity-conserving practices like living in the moment and maintaining normalcy. That can seem impossible at times, but there will be a moment in every day when these methods will sustain both the dying person and the caregiver.

It's also the time to remind the dying person they are beautiful (or handsome) to you and that you love them. If you can't think of how to say that out loud, try making a joke of it the first time. Tell them "I read in this book that it's important I tell you that you are beautiful to me and that I love you. So here goes: 'You are beautiful, and I love you!'" Once you've said it the first time, repeat it routinely. It may be tough at first to say these words out loud, but it gets more comfortable with practice. It also may be funny to mention it in the middle of an unusually intimate and uncomfortable moment, that is, if you can say it with love and it's in line with the dying person's sense of humor.

As awkward as it can be, the intimacy that develops by assisting a person with the daily activities of self-care provides a unique opportunity to work past the superficial and on to what matters. It may be helpful to remember that you are caring for someone you love when they need you the most.

The caregiver is often tuned in to even minor changes because they are with the dying person so much. Most changes will be the natural progression of the illness, but sometimes there is a complication that accelerates a decline. If you see a sudden change, don't hesitate to consult with your hospice team. Establish a communication pattern with them to get the support both you and the dying person need. The hospice team is getting paid daily to support you and your family. Take advantage of this resource with regular communication.

Communicate to family, friends, and members of the hospice team how you want to be informed of their visits (e.g., a call at a specific time or a certain amount of minutes before they arrive). The hospice team's schedule can change due to the nature of the work, but a call when they are on their way will keep you from waiting for their arrival.

There may be times when the dying person becomes confused. This can be because they are distracted or due to the effect of medications, or it could be related to physical decline. Discuss what you've observed with the hospice team.

The caregiver is also often distracted, with their expanding role, among other things. Use a journal to write down topics you want to discuss during hospice calls or visits. Many hospice teams provide a journal as part of their care. Journaling regularly with dates and times will help keep thoughts straight. If the dying person is taking opioids to control pain, keep a log of when they are taking them. This will give the nurse and doctor information on how to adjust pain and other medications.

It's also time to revisit the circles of support. As the caregiver role expands, support is critical. Make sure you've got requests ready so when people ask, you can tell them exactly what will help. If they don't ask, reach out with specific requests. Most people want to help.

Ask for instructions from the hospice team regarding assisting the dying person in their daily activities. Ask specifically about each one: locomotion (moving around), transfers, movement in bed, dressing, feeding, personal hygiene, and toileting. The hospice team has effective practices, tricks, and equipment for each. The sooner you are familiar with them and start using them, the more comfortable your job will be.

Don't risk exhaustion. Prioritize self-care. The process of dying is often more of a marathon than a sprint. If self-care breaks down during this phase, it will be tough to recover during the next phases. The caregiver practices self-care so they can be there to support their loved one through it all.

It is not uncommon for a caregiver to become ill shortly after the death of their loved one. Knowing this, now is the time to schedule an appointment with your doctor. Let them know what's going on in your life and ask for their support in keeping you healthy. Make a plan to have an appointment or to call and check in shortly after the death occurs to address your needs at that time too.

Hospice volunteers and therapists provide a vital, nonmedical form of support. Many hospices offer services like massage, art, pet, or music therapy. Some assist in creating legacy documents like letters to children, videos, or life reviews. Hospice therapists and volunteers provide moments of respite, relief, companionship, and fun. Seek out volunteer or other services from your hospice or circles of support.

Honor alone time. Unless the dying person is someone who insists or needs the constant presence of people, give them some space. Create time where you are out of the room if possible. Assure them you are within earshot and let them be alone. Provide a bell to summon assistance. Have fun with it if you can. There will likely be a time when you miss the sound of the bell. If possible, cherish each ring.

Assess how you are doing with the Eight Dimensions of Wellness in the Assisting Phase.

1. Physical - Are you exercising, eating healthy foods, and sleeping enough?
2. Occupational – How am I managing daily work with caregiving at this point?
3. Intellectual – Am I accessing needed resources?
4. Financial – Are there any financial or legal issues to resolve?
5. Social – Am I staying in touch with people and avoiding isolation?
6. Environmental – How is the environment supporting my well-being?
7. Spiritual – Who is my spiritual support? Am I in touch with them?

8. Emotional – Who is supporting my emotional needs at this point? Are we talking about what's happening or keeping it inside?

If the answers to these questions are troubling, seek out a social worker. They are trained in finding resources and in counseling people through difficult times.

Look at the list above and each day ask, "What can I do today that's good for me?" It doesn't have to be big. Call a friend. Touch base with work. Meditate or pray. Ask for help. Take a walk. Scream into a pillow. Cry. Exercise. Laugh. Journal.

The Family

If possible, it's time to offer help now. If the caregiver doesn't provide direction, let them know what you will be doing and then do it. See the sidebar for examples.

The caregiver's caregiver should start regular check-ins during the Assisting phase. Put it on the calendar and do it. If possible, visit regularly so you can look for ways to be supportive. If they don't need help, then just be there. You can adjust the frequency of visits based on the growing need and their feedback. Honor the caregiver's wishes.

Don't Ask. Make an Offer and Deliver. I'll…

- bring dinner on Tuesday.
- take you both for a ride on Friday.
- mow the lawn on Saturday.
- do grocery shopping every Thursday. I'll call Wednesday night for your list.
- stay with Dad while you do your weekly shopping/exercise/have lunch with friends.
- call you every Sunday at 4 p.m. to see how you're doing.
- spend the night on weekends so you can get some uninterrupted sleep time.
- help on shower days.
- do laundry on Tuesdays and Saturdays.
- get the dog groomed or clean the kitty litter.

Alternatively, depending on the size of the family and circle of friends, it may be time to step back a bit. The dying person will likely have good and bad days. They may be spending more time sleeping. Visit lengths should be adjusted as needed. The dying person and caregiver may guide others in how they spend both good and bad days. If they don't, the family should assess and adjust. Pay attention to more than just words.

At the same time, if there are unresolved issues or things that need attention, be upfront about it. The hospice team includes a doctor, nurse, social worker, chaplain, therapists, and volunteers. They are there to support the whole family. Reach out to them for help in figuring out an approach. They are part of the team to assist you through this process.

If you can be involved (with your presence, your prayers, your help, or your interaction) at any point after someone has been given the news they are dying, you will give and get a great gift.

The Environment

Consider what changes in the environment are needed now. Is it time for a hospital bed to be brought in? These beds offer many useful features. They adjust up and down to sitting and lying positions and can be moved around a room relatively easily. They also have waterproof mattresses. If the dying person and caregiver are sleeping in the same bed, consider the impact on the caregiver's ability to get a good night's sleep. There is room in a hospital bed for cuddle time and sleeping in separate beds may be the key to the caregiver's well-being.

Assess regularly what adjustments may be needed for the senses. Don't be surprised if the dying person becomes less or more opinionated about them. In the next phases, the dying person will likely be less concerned about daily decisions and will take on more of a veto role. As this occurs, expand your "sense review" to support both the dying person and the caregiver. See Appendix E (The Senses).

Talk to your hospice team about any environmental issues that come up.

For a quick reference outlining this phase, go to Appendix C (PACE Checklist).

Chapter 3

Caring

CARING is the phase where the caregiver makes most, if not all, decisions and is responsible for making all daily activities happen.

The Caring phase marks two significant changes. First, the dying person is often less interested in control or in making decisions because they are beginning the process of turning inward, or they are physically or mentally no longer capable of being in control.

The second change is that the caregiver now takes on the full-time job of providing care. Whether these changes happen gradually or rapidly, there can be less mental angst around the changing roles as with previous phases just because there is no other choice.

Still, there isn't a specific moment in time when the transition happens. Parts of each phase often flow into the next. There will be a time, though, when it becomes clear you are in the Caring phase.

The Dying Person

The dying person may still be concerned about their modesty, but as their energy reserves decrease, priorities move toward what is most important at the moment, e.g., moving around, toileting, getting rest.

There may also still be resistance to accepting needed help, and as a result, there could be safety issues that come up (e.g., falling). As the need for help increases, eventually so does the acceptance. A pad, diaper, or catheter may seem intolerable at first, but getting up to go to the bathroom can also become too much. Deciding which one will work better and when depends on the person and the situation.

The dying person's thinking may be clear at one point and distracted or uninterested at other times. Facts mean less. Social norms mean even less. Routines will end, and others that reflect short-term needs will begin.

It is during this phase where the dying person is dependent on others for all activities of their daily life. They will need assistance for all transitions from the bed to the bathroom or bedside commode or chair, etc. See Appendix D (Activities of Daily Living [ADLs]) for more information.

During the Caring phase, it is rare for an outing to occur. Instead, there are more sleep or rest filled days.

"It's too much!"

Explaining takes energy. A friend told me about how her mother, who was always a strong-willed person, could communicate without a long-winded explanation. Her mom would occasionally indicate she was no longer interested in whatever was going on by saying, "It's too much!" One day, they were at the mall when she said it. Without a word, the family knew to head to the car.

Our family has now adopted this line as the one to use when anyone has had it. The words deliver a clear message but with humor, and no more talking (or energy) is needed. Utilizing a catchphrase like, "It's too much!" to communicate a real need can be a clear and concise signal to stop, without having to explain anymore.

A note about pain during this phase and as death approaches: not everyone has to deal with pain as they die. It depends on many factors, including which disease is the cause of death. A general rule is that if someone has not been in pain in the past, they will not likely be in pain as they die, and vice versa. Of course, this may not be true for everyone.

The Caregiver

Changing roles may affect the caregiver more than the dying person during the Caring phase. The caregiver may be worried about their ability to provide care to the end. It may be helpful to explore worries as objectively as possible and consider options. If it's culturally acceptable to you, consider enlisting outside providers, family, or friends for the care you are not able to provide physically or emotionally. For instance, it's okay if you can't or don't want to bathe your parent. Talk with them about the options and if possible, decide together. If not, it's your call. Err on the side of obtaining too much help during this phase to conserve energy. You can always change your mind. If you're interested but your family cannot afford paid caregivers, talk to a social worker about options.

Assistance can mean help with chores around the house or having someone stay with the dying person, providing time for the caregiver to take a walk or run errands. The caregiver should leave the bedside--and home, routinely. Even if it feels like you are the only person who can provide caregiving, it's not true. You will remain the primary caregiver and be better at it, but allowing others to participate directly will provide needed breaks.

Start or increase communication with the circles of support. In most cases, it will be beneficial to share what's going on now and what is concerning. Communicate what's needed for you to be able to remain the primary caregiver and tell others what worries you most.

Solutions could mean bringing additional part-time help in, or for 24 hours a day. It could mean moving the dying person to a friend or relative's home, to a nursing home with hospice, or to a hospice house. Regardless, when most people make the decision, they wish they had done it sooner. The hospice social worker can help work through affordable options.

Talk to the hospice team about respite care. Respite care means paid professionals provide care to the dying person so the regular caregiver can rest or take care of business (e.g., the caregiver may be exhausted and need sleep, or they may need to leave town for a few days). Care is provided by a skilled nursing facility. Respite care includes everything the dying person needs for a short amount of time. It provides relief for the primary caregivers for a few hours per week up to five days depending on the situation. Respite care is paid for with some insurance plans when a person is in hospice, but there are limits. Learn how to use it ahead of time, so you know how to make it happen when it's needed.

Look to your caregiver (the caregiver's caregiver) for support and as a sounding board. If they are available, take advantage of their help to take some time for yourself. Take a break when you can with the help of family or friends.

The mental state of the dying person can change during the Caring phase. Be aware if the dying person is uncooperative or combative. Abusive or unsafe behavior can appear suddenly, especially with diseases that affect the brain, including dementia. Uncharacteristic behavior can also be caused by infection or by medications. Note trends in the type of behavior you are witnessing (e.g., time of day, activity). Use your journal for this and alert your hospice team to this or any change in behavior (e.g., sleeping in the day and being awake at night). Changes in behavior may signal an issue that needs to be addressed.

Words matter, and they need to be put in perspective. If the dying person says things that hurt your feelings, talk to your hospice team about it. If you say or feel like saying things to the dying person that will upset them, talk to your hospice team about it. They can help you work through what is happening and create a plan that will serve both you and the dying person well. It's normal for everyone involved to reach the end of their rope during this phase. Seeking out support when it happens is a healthy way to deal with it.

Slowing down and not rushing can also help make everyone feel at ease and achieve tasks calmly. Taking time to talk and explain what is happening to the dying person, even if it has to be repeated several times a day, can be helpful to reduce resistance and avoid confrontation.

It is helpful to others for the caregiver to arrange for and offer time alone with the dying person for individuals in your circle of friends and family during this phase too. The caregiver's presence is comforting, but it can also stop people from having private discussions that could benefit everyone. Caregivers can look for excuses to announce they will be out of the room and then provide privacy—even for 10 or

15 minutes. Assess the room when you return. Offer support to both the visitor and dying person.

Offer support to both the visitor and dying person.

- "This is a difficult time, and I see it's hard on both of you."
- "I know there's a lot to work through. You are both brave to talk about it."
- "I love you both, and I'm proud you're here together."

Of course, if the dying person requests not to be left alone with someone, then you should honor their wishes.

Caregivers should also be aware that there is no timeline to the Caring phase. It can last a long while. Pace yourself. At this point, your loved one, the dying person, is your patient. You are a full- time, full-fledged caregiver. This can be very scary for people who have obligations outside the home, like a job. It is now time to call for reinforcements. Be objective about your abilities. Take care of yourself, so you can take care of others.

Note that it is not uncommon for people to live longer than six months while receiving hospice care. It speaks to how effective hospice care is for meeting the needs of the dying person. When this happens, hospice can be continued if there is evidence that the dying person is continuing to decline (e.g., losing weight, becoming more confused, sleeping more, experiencing increased pain, becoming more dependent).

Re-assess the environment to assure you have the equipment and knowledge to keep you both safe and comfortable. There are tools available to assist in moving a person in bed and between the bed and a chair, or to a wheelchair or bedside commode. Your hospice team will guide you, but they will be able to help more if you tell them what's happening.

After you get the equipment you need, ask for training in how to use it. Do this even if the dying person is not in full agreement. You cannot take care of them if you are injured. And if you can't move them safely, let your hospice team know and consider other options. Review the Appendix D (Activities of Daily Living [ADLs]) for more information on tools and equipment.

Pain Management

Be proactive with pain management. If moving hurts (e.g., when transferring from the bed to a chair), give pain medication 30-60 minutes (or whatever time frame it takes for the medication to work) before the planned move.

Look for nonverbal signs of pain (e.g., grimacing, irritability, restlessness, and arm or leg movement). If the caregiver suspects pain is getting worse, communicate what's observed to the hospice team.

Managing pain or shortness of breath and constipation can become one of the caregiver's major roles during this phase. Pain, shortness of breath, and constipation make people feel miserable. Opioids are invaluable for increasing quality of life for many people during this phase, but when they cause painful constipation, they reduce the quality of life. This point can't be stressed enough. Medications that support regularity should be given with opioids from the start and increased as opioids are increased. Medical professionals call the management of constipation a "bowel regimen." Note that medication to fight constipation may change as the digestive tract slows. Laxatives may be more useful than stool softeners because they stimulate the bowels. Work with your hospice team on this.

Opioids Cause Constipation

Opioids reduce the movement of the intestines and increase the reabsorption of water from the feces into the lining of the intestine resulting in slow-moving, dry feces.

To avoid constipation, make sure these all happen:

- Start using a laxative (e.g., Senna S, Milk of Magnesia) when an opioid is started. A stool softener is not enough. Note: A laxative stimulates the colon. A stool softener makes the stool softer.

- Increase laxatives as dosages are increased.

- Increase fluid intake if possible.

- Try "the brown bomb": warm prune juice along with a laxative if constipation occurs.

- Everyone has a different pattern. If their pattern changes, a plan to get them back on track should be put in place. A rule of thumb is that no one should go more than three days without a bowel movement.

- Consult your hospice team with any questions about above.

Note: As the dying person slows and then stops eating, their stool output will decrease but it shouldn't stop.

Another note on opioids. They have a well-deserved bad reputation, but for relieving symptoms at end of life, they are the drug of choice because they are effective and safe. Do your research and ask enough questions so you can get comfortable with their use. Then learn how to dispose of any leftover medication. Or read the next paragraph.

The FDA recommends a four-step process for disposing of unused medications:1) Mix medicines (do not crush tablets or capsules) with an unpalatable substance such as dirt, cat litter, or used coffee grounds, 2) Place the mixture in a container such as a sealed plastic bag or milk container, 3) Throw the container in your household trash, and 4) Delete all personal information on the prescription label of empty pill bottles or medicine packaging, then dispose of the container in the trash. There are also local programs that provide for the disposal of drugs.

The Family

Ideally, there has been a communication pattern established, so the family is aware that caregiving is now full time and will likely take more than one person. If not, it is time for regular communication, and it's time for the family to offer help and to check in on the level of care needed.

There is always an update to give, but the caregiver may be too tired to think about what to share. See the sidebar for sample questions.

Sample Questions to Ask the Caregiver:

- Is the dying person sleeping through the night? Are you?
- Are you able to bathe them? Are you able to take a shower/bath when you want?
- Are they eating one, two, or three meals a day? Are you?
- How is their pain? Are you in any pain?
- Are you able to keep up with laundry, grocery shopping, cooking, and errands?
- Is there yard work or other seasonal chores that need doing?

Pause for longer than you think. Give them time to answer.

Be careful not to judge or offer unsolicited advice.

Listening to their answers will provide an idea of what additional help may be needed.

This phase is also a good time for meaningful visits and conversations with the dying person, although you should watch for clues about their energy level and adjust accordingly. Their energy level will decrease during this phase, or their energy could be high one day/hour and low the next.

Now is the time for the family to start (or even better, to continue) to support the caregiver's decisions. It is not the details of day-to-day decisions that matter most when a loved one is dying. It is that the people involved support one another. Suggestions are okay if they are 1) asked for, 2) helpful with stated goals like comfort, or 3) about a definite safety issue. Resist giving suggestions as much as possible and avoid critiques. Consciously replace both with compliments or observations.

"You are good at caregiving."

"I can see how much you love them."

"I know this can't be easy, and you are providing what they need right now."

"This is obviously not easy. I want to help. I will…

After any of these comments, stop and listen. Practice counting to ten silently before replying. It may even take longer for their answer to form. When they do respond, try to hear the meaning beyond their words.

If the caregiver seems stuck on a problem and you have a suggestion, ask permission to share your thoughts. For example, "My friend had a similar issue. Would you like to hear what they learned from it?"

Use this guideline: if you aren't willing or able to step in and do what you are about to advise, then don't advise.

Increase support but don't smother. The Caring phase is often longer than people expect. It can last for months. Now is a great time to visit and stay for a while. Give the caregiver a break. Ask for alone time if you want it. Visiting is an opportunity to reconcile, entertain, or distract, and to say what needs to be said. A bonus is that visitors will know they contributed to the dying person's care.

Any family member who takes on an active, regular role in caregiving should consider connecting with the hospice team. The new caregiver can ask to be present when hospice team members visit or can call the case manager to introduce themselves.

Arrange for little luxuries (fresh flowers, candles [but not if oxygen is being used], an in-home hairdresser or in-home massage, nail and pedicure for the patient and caregiver) until they decline them. Be aware that efforts regarding appearance should also be moving toward comfort. Hair maintenance is terrific if it feels good but not as crucial if it causes discomfort. Beauty now comes in the form of being in the presence of one another.

Maintain the dying person's modesty and dignity (e.g., provide privacy when requested, call before each visit, ask how long you can stay), and verbalize kind and compassionate compliments in every direction.

The Environment

Review how the environment can support the caregiver and dying person. Room layout and equipment can be changed throughout this phase to meet changing needs.

Bed sores (also known as pressure ulcers) are common and a concern if the dying person's circulation is compromised and/or if they are remaining in the same position for long periods. A turning schedule (2-3 hours), pillows, wedges, mattresses that alternate pressure, skin care creams, sprays, and moisture barrier supplies can help. Inform your hospice team immediately if you see a red or dark spot on the dying person's skin, especially on the places that make contact with the bed or chair (e.g., lower back and buttocks, heels, hips, elbows, shoulders, ears, and back of head). Most bed sores/pressure ulcers are preventable and can be stopped if caught early.

Cleaning spills and cleaning up body fluids may be necessary during this phase. Having cleaning supplies at the ready will pay off. Dark towels hide stubborn stains. For effective infection prevention, read the directions on products to get the full disinfectant benefit (e.g., generally, cleaners provide the most disinfecting benefits if surfaces air-dry).

Questions to prompt ideas:

- Is the home or somewhere else the best place for this phase?
- Is the room arranged in a way that is helpful and safe (e.g., access to both sides of the hospital bed).
- If they want to, can the dying person see out the window?
- What is the view from the dying person's perspective, including what does the ceiling look like?
- Are there stable/sturdy arms on chairs to provide leverage and support when trying to stand?

- Are there grab bars or solid support if needed to walk around the room?
- Is clutter regularly reduced as much as possible?
- Can we get folding chairs for visitors and put them away when they aren't needed?
- What toileting routine works best for now?
- Would equipment like a hospital bed or bedside commode be helpful now?

Hint: A hospital bedside table (also known as an overbed table) is useful in many ways—even as a laptop table when sitting on a couch. The hospice team will use it when providing a bed bath or other procedures and the rollers and adjustable height make it a worthwhile convenience to have one on hand.

For a quick reference outlining this phase go to Appendix C (PACE Checklist).

Chapter 4

Ending

ENDING is the phase that describes when the dying person completely disengages with this world, and the caregiver remains in the decision-making role and is responsible for all decisions and work.

This phase is also known as "transitioning" or "actively dying." It is the proverbial "death-bed." It means death is imminent, but as we said before, there is never an exact, predictable timetable. The Ending phase can go on for hours, days, or more than a week, sometimes two or more.

As the journey comes to an end, there are a few things to keep top of mind.

First, no one dies in exactly the same way. Many people cope with the uncertainty of the dying process by predicting—comparing or looking for signs of the next part of the process. This is normal, but none of the signs change the fact that the dying person will die when they do. There is no precise predictable or "normal" way for death to occur. The dying person or caregiver may have made plans for these final moments, but there is little chance that all will go as planned. Furthermore, trying to stick to the plan at all costs is not helpful. Expecting the unexpected with flexibility and acceptance as death nears will make it easier for everyone involved. Broader goals, like comfort (for everyone) as the priority, will be more achievable than specific goals.

Second, as a society, we have not talked about the death process openly, so for many, it's tough to know precisely how we should approach it. The good news is that knowing there is not a set pattern can be freeing. No matter how it goes—messy or neat, noisy or quiet, slow or fast, as planned or entirely unpredictably—by witnessing death, you are observing and participating in one of the most natural parts of life.

The Dying Person

During this phase the dying person is turning inward, sleeping more, and eating less. They are entirely dependent on caregivers. The dying person will likely have less interest in stimuli like music, TV, or visitors. They may say things that are confusing or even hurtful. Social norms mean little to them during this phase. They may not be concerned about dignity but obviously still deserve it.

Swallowing becomes difficult or impossible. If there is pain, it may be communicated verbally but will more likely be observed through the dying person grimacing or moaning, or showing agitation or restlessness. Coughing can occur. Urinary incontinence or retention (not being able to urinate) can also occur. Work with your hospice team to create a plan for these issues.

Some people have "visions"—seeing and talking to people who aren't there, often people who have already passed on. These "visions" are normal for someone who is dying, and many people who have witnessed this experience note that the they often bring the dying person comfort.

We can't say for sure what the experience of gradual death is like, but we have no reason to believe that death in and of itself is painful. If the disease process causes pain or other unpleasant sensations, medications can usually manage the symptoms. Pain medications can increase sleep, but sleep time increases without medications too.

As death nears, any of these observations are normal. None of them are thought to be uncomfortable for the dying person. As a person dies, their body no longer serves them as it did when they were alive and changes occur. For instance:

- Appetite decreases and then goes away.
- Weakness increases.
- More sleep occurs.
- Confusion or restlessness can occur.
- The systems in the body (e.g., digestion, circulation) slow and then shut down.
- Skin can become itchy as kidneys shut down.
- Mottling or purple blotches may appear on various parts of the body.
- Limbs lose feeling as the body prioritizes the preservation of the heart and brain. This process is not believed to be uncomfortable for the dying person. Fingers and toes may turn gray or blue, or may feel cold to the touch.
- Limbs sometimes swell.
- Temperature regulation stops, and the dying person may or may not want to be covered. Shivering is the body's reaction to cold. There may be a fever. If the dying person moves their arms repeatedly, they may be trying to remove or pull up blankets.
- Breathing becomes irregular, often with very long pauses in between. Breathing can also be noisy, and sound like snoring.

- Lips can turn purple or black for periods of time. This can be alarming, but knowing it is a normal part of the dying process can be helpful.
- The dying person may not awaken to voice or touch.
- Senses like sight, smell, taste, and touch are diminished and stop. Hearing is believed to be the last sense to cease.
- The pulse becomes weak.
- Eyes can be teary, opened, or half opened.
- When breathing is irregular, the moment of death is often uncertain. It may take a few minutes of noticing a lack of breath to be sure that death has occurred.

The Caregiver

If possible, this phase is when there should be more than one caregiver around the clock. The primary caregiver should remain ultimately in charge but also may welcome sharing the work and responsibility.

All caregivers can offer support to the dying person by considering the following:
- Partner with your hospice team to review what to expect and to have a plan for how to address any issues that come up.

- Allow for food and drink to decrease and stop based on the dying person's cues. Feeding the dying person is comforting to the living, not the dying. The dying person may like a taste but will likely not eat much. They may even eat just to comfort their caregiver. Food is no longer useful and will not process as their digestive system shuts down. This change is a hard one for all of us. Food has meant comfort to us all our lives, but it may help to know that providing unneeded liquids can increase noisy breathing as they die.
- Reading out loud, talking, praying, playing music, or just being present, are other ways to provide support and comfort.
- Mouth care can continue with a wet cloth or mouth swab (it looks like a lollipop with a small sponge on the end.).
- For many dying people, swallowing can be difficult during this phase. Work with your hospice team on how to address it if this is an issue. Some medications are given with a patch or as liquid under the tongue (sublingual), so they are easier to swallow than a pill.
- If the dying person becomes disoriented, seeing and talking to someone that isn't

apparent to you, provide quiet support. Don't argue or correct them. If they become agitated by the visions, distract them by noting your presence and where they are and letting them know they are safe and you are near.

- If the dying person says something hurtful, talk to your hospice team or friends who have been through this. They will provide you with reassurance that this is normal, and they will help you deal with it.
- If the dying person is short of breath, talk to your hospice team immediately. A small fan blowing gently toward their face, raising the head of the bed, and keeping the room cool can help. Medications like morphine can decrease the sensation of shortness of breath, providing comfort. Oxygen helps, but don't adjust oxygen without consulting your hospice team. No open flames nearby—cigarettes, candles, gas stoves when oxygen is in use.
- Address pain based on the dying person's wishes and the cues you observe. Do not be afraid to increase medications as prescribed. Comfort is the goal. You will not kill them. The disease or condition they have is the cause of their death. On the other hand, sometimes

pain medications are no longer needed. Observe the dying person for signs of pain or no pain. Talk to your hospice team for reassurance regarding pain medications.

- Continue to bathe and apply lotion if the ending phase lasts days or weeks.
- Continue to reposition (every 3 to 5 hours) but not at the expense of the comfort of the dying person. Adding pillows and slight adjustments can replace complete repositioning. Some hospice professionals think death often occurs shortly after repositioning, so they delay repositions for when key family members are present.
- If it is painful for the dying person to move, schedule pain medications 30 minutes before moves. Regardless, the dying person may still show signs they don't like to be moved, but hygiene is still important and it doesn't take long. If you're tempted to say, "I'm sorry." while moving the patient, replace it with, "I love you." You are showing your love through your care. Matching your actions with words reminds everyone of the love in your actions.
- Place absorbent pads under the dying person. At the time of death, bowels and bladder relax so fluids may release.

- Holding hands can provide comfort, but a gentle touch to the dying person's chest may be felt more by them as their body systems shut down and blood flow concentrates between the heart and brain.
- The hearing sense is believed to be the last to shut down. Continue to talk to the dying person, not above them or about them as if they are not in the room, even after death.

Caregivers can offer support for themselves, their family, and friends by:
- Communicating to their circles of support, even if it is to tell them you won't be communicating again until after the death.
- Using respite care as needed without guilt. Many caregivers feel they must do it all and then are so exhausted at the end, they can't be physically or mentally present, Ask the hospice team about respite care.
- Creating an environment that is supportive of both the dying person and you.
- Considering soft music, a small fan to keep air circulating, and background noise or aromatherapy.
- Inviting those whom you or the dying person need to be there at a certain stage or time.

Be clear on how long you want them to stay and consider their needs, too.

- Taking shifts. This phase of dying, like all the rest, is not predictable and can go on for days or a week, two or more.
- Offering and providing alone time for family and friends. This time can give the caregiver breaks and genuinely involve others in the process.
- Following the dying person's wishes, but do not harm yourself. If it becomes too much, turn to your hospice team for guidance.
- Knowing it is entirely reasonable to hope death will occur soon. Many people do at some point in the process. If you feel distressed by this thought, share it with the hospice team. You will receive reassurance that this is very normal and is a human response to the process.
- Don't be afraid to leave the dying person alone for short amounts of time. There is some speculation that dying people sometimes wait to be alone to die. We can't be sure about that, but know that it's okay to leave the room for awhile.
- Embracing hugs (pun intended) from anyone who offers—if it is comforting to you. This physical expression of support can bolster

your reserves, along with sleep, regular
healthy eating, and exercise.

The Family

Anyone who is concerned about being with the
person at the time of death should be present now.
It is often not possible for everyone to be present
at the bedside at the exact moment of death, yet
some people stress out over it. It's helpful to reframe
expectations so that being involved in any part of
the dying process is "being present." In other words,
anyone engaged in the Caring or Ending phases is
present in the dying process.

Family and friends can help most now by supporting
the primary caregiver in their role. This is especially true for those who have not been present in
all phases of the dying process. Support the decisions the caregiver has made and is making. Do not
second guess unless there is risk of serious harm. Tell
them repeatedly they are doing a good job.

If possible, offer and then provide support unless
it's declined (e.g., sitting with the dying person,
organizing supplies, cleaning up the house, doing
laundry).

Show affection. If it is culturally acceptable, hug everyone involved (caregiver, family, friends, hospice team, etc.) often.

A Few Phrases to Inspire You

- You mean so much to me.
- I will miss you so much, but your lessons will stay with me.
- You've taught me well.
- Thank you for being such a wonderful parent/sister/wife/partner.
- You are so handsome/beautiful to me.
- I remember when…
- I love you.
- I ask for your forgiveness.
- I hope you forgive me.
- I forgive you.
- Thank you.

Some conversations with the dying person may still be possible if you catch them at the right time. Regardless, it is never too late to say what you want to say to them. It is never too late to reconcile, even if there is no feedback from the dying person. Talking to the body after death is also encouraged.

If you are at a loss for words, consider reading poems or prayers, or singing and playing an instrument. The sound of your voice or music may bring comfort.

Ask for alone time with the dying person if desired. This can double as a break for the caregiver. It might not be comfortable for some people to be alone with a dying person, but it will likely be a cherished moment to look back on. Determine how long you stay based on your ability and the caregiver's needs. Your visit could give the caregiver a few minutes to take a nap or take care of a need, or it could become intrusive if the visit lasts too long.

Assemble a caregiver kit/care package to deliver during a visit, and include items like magazines, a gift card and delivery service from a neighborhood restaurant, favorite snacks, bottled water, a smoothie, special tea or coffee, favorite music, lotion—whatever the caregiver likes.

The Environment

Create a comforting sensory environment for everyone.

Rearrange the room with comfortable chairs. Bring out folding chairs when needed and move them out of the way when visitors leave. Provide healthy food and drink for the caregiver and visitors.

Remove items from the room including any patient equipment that is no longer needed (bedside commode, walker, cane) to minimize clutter and reduce the risk of visitors or caregivers tripping and falling.

Be careful when carrying trays or arm loads of things that may block the view of the walking path to prevent tripping over something on the floor.

There should be an increasing focus on the caregiver's needs in this phase. Use proper body mechanics when moving the dying person. Your hospice team can teach you tricks to help (e.g., raise the hospital bed to waist height when moving the dying person or providing care, use a draw sheet and have two people perform moves).

Pillows and wedges (pillow-sized, triangular-shaped foam pieces) can be used to hold the dying person in a new position. Your hospice team will provide them.

After Death Occurs

After death, the preparation completed months and weeks before pays off.

Take the time to sit quietly with the person who has died for a few minutes. Note that their life has ended, and you were there as a witness to their passing. This moment is a once-in-a-lifetime event, for all of you. Taking time to be present at that moment will help you recall the honor and privilege the moment deserves.

When you are ready, notify the hospice team that death has occurred and confirm next steps. Notify any family or friends who need to bear witness to the death. If you want, let those closest to the person who has died decide if they wish to spend time with or be involved in preparing the body. Trust their instincts. Some people regret not having the experience, but few regret having it.

If you are comfortable doing so, talk with your hospice team ahead of time about how involved you want to be in preparing the body. These professionals can help with education, assistance, and supplies.

Religious or cultural practices provide guidelines for preparing a body after death. The hospice team does the same. Below are some general things to know.

Since rigor mortis can happen within hours, the following practices can help keep the body in a natural position.

- Close the eyes. Place a smooth, folded cloth over them. A small plastic bag with rice or seeds can be used as a lightweight way to keep eyes closed. The eyes will stay shut without anything on them after some time has passed.

- Do not remove dentures. It will be hard to replace them after rigor mortis begins.
- Position the head to keep the mouth closed. If needed, tie a scarf or ACE™ Elastic Bandage around the head, supporting the chin for a few hours.
- Position the body flat with arms at sides and legs straight.
- Washing the body may take two or more people. It is very similar to cleaning a person in bed. Essential oils are a commonly used rinse.
- Keep the body covered in a light blanket or sheet after cleaning to preserve dignity.
- Keep the room cool with air conditioning, a fan, or open window to preserve the body.
- Soft lighting, soft music, candles, or essential oils can help create an atmosphere of respect and honor.
- Hospice equipment (e.g. bed, table, oxygen) is routinely picked up the next working day.

Medication Disposal

It is critically important that leftover medications are safely disposed of. Your hospice will guide you through how to do this, or a pharmacist can be consulted ahead of time for guidance. Many pharmacies will provide you with a free disposal kit. It's easy to use. Disposing of leftover medications (especially opioids) properly is a way to protect the environment and quite possibly save a life.

The FDA recommends a four-step process for disposing of unused medications: 1) Mix medicines (do not crush tablets or capsules) with an unpalatable substance such as dirt, cat litter, or used coffee grounds, 2) Place the mixture in a container such as a sealed plastic bag or milk container, 3) Throw the container in your household trash, and 4) Delete all personal information on the prescription label of empty pill bottles or medicine packaging, then dispose of the container in the trash. There are also local programs that provide for the disposal of drugs.

Bereavement

One of the best parts of hospice care is bereavement support. Hospice teams have the training and experience to provide guidance through a difficult and often confusing time. They have people on staff who have been trained in providing bereavement support. They can tell you what's normal behavior and can provide education and guidance on how to recognize and what to do about behavior that requires additional support.

Bereavement support is for the caregiver AND family. Children, siblings, or grandchildren are not routinely in touch with the hospice team, so those who are in touch must provide the connection. If there is anyone in the family who is struggling, ask your hospice team to talk to their bereavement specialist about the situation early to avoid more significant issues later.

Bereavement support is typically available to the caregiver and family for up to a year after the death and sometimes indefinitely. Take advantage of it. A simple phone call to discuss whatever is going on can provide needed reassurance or a referral to needed expert care.

For a quick reference outlining this phase go to Appendix C (PACE Checklist).

Essence

Essence can be defined as the intrinsic nature or indispensable quality of something, especially something abstract, that determines its character.

Synonyms for essence include quintessence, soul, spirit, nature, core, heart, crux, and nucleus. For most of us, there are few times in life when the essence of a person is all that matters. Birth and death both provide a moment in time when a life comes clearly into view in its complexity, pureness, and wonder.

Being present as a child takes their first breath gives us a unique perspective on this amazing thing called life. The child wasn't here nine months ago and yet, here they are, a human being, beginning their journey of life. How glorious it is. How lucky we are to experience that moment with them. We don't know who they will be or what they will encounter in their life, but that doesn't matter. It is our witness to their birth and our presence with them that matters at this moment.

Being with a dying person as they transition from this life brings a similar focus on the essence of the person. There is little space for the mundane thoughts of everyday life. What matters now is this person, this human being who has lived a life that is now ending. If you have had the privilege to go through life with this person you will know what was important to them in earlier phases of their life and during the death process. Feel honor in the knowledge that you were allowed insight into the essence of their being as they made their way through this transition. You've been given the opportunity to understand the essential things that made them the person they were, and you've been given the chance to see firsthand the mysterious transition from life to death.

If you did not go through life with this person or don't know them well, witnessing their death is still profound. You may not know much about who they were in life, but you will know their essence in the time you spent with them and their impact on you. In addition, you will know you provided them with comfort and dignity through their transition.

This one moment in time provides us with the opportunity to reflect on and honor the dying person's essence. Their nature, soul, and substance is their legacy. At the end of this life, what remains behind is the impact they've had on others and on our world. This human being has been here on this earth since they were born. They've lived their life. And then, at the end of one breath, they are no longer here. As witnesses, we are honored to be present to the miracle of this person at this point in their journey. It is their essence and our presence with them during this transition that matters in this moment.

For many religious and spiritual people, there are rituals to honor the transition from life to death. Most involve acknowledging the individual and their place in something that is bigger than one person. Many who spend time with the dying are profoundly impacted by what they witness. Perhaps it is because of something larger that connects us all and during this transition, our connection to one another becomes clearer. When we take what we've learned from this experience and use it to bring a new perspective to our own lives, the impact of the dying person continues on.

As humans we search for meaning in our experiences, sometimes finding it and other times, not finding it with clear success. The transition from life to death is no different. Acknowledging and honoring a person's essence provides us with a fresh view of the wonder and awe of life.

Final Thought

Everyone who lives into adulthood has a final six months of life. As more of us die gradually, accepting that fact provides us with the chance to make the time of transition as meaningful as the months before birth. Recognizing and understanding the changes that will occur can provide us with opportunities to show love, mend relationships, and make peace with our lives and our deaths.

It is our hope that this book will provide people with enough information to increase their ability to support one another during the death process, to start conversations, to promote the comfort of everyone involved, and to celebrate the life, death, and the essence of the dying person.

Appendix A (PACE Mnemonic)

	Stage	Dying person	Caregiver	Family	Environment
P	Partnering	Engages in decision making and daily work.	Works equally with dying person regarding decisions and daily work.	Visits dying person. Considers becoming the caregiver's caregiver. Appreciates and supports caregiver.	Assess environment and align with dying person's wishes. Consider safety for dying person and caregiver.
A	Assisting	Allows or asks the caregiver to help with day-to-day work and decisions.	Looks to dying person for preferences, but makes more decisions and does more of the day-to-day work.	Offers help. Checks in with caregiver from time to time. Visits regularly and seeks out ways to be supportive.	Reassess environment. Consider hospital bed or equipment. Do a sensory review for both dying person and caregiver.
C	Caring	Has little involvement in decisions and day-to-day work.	Takes on decision-making role and day-to-day work entirely.	Visits dying person. Supports and complements caregiver. Resists critique.	Make changes to support everyone (e.g., lighting, clutter, chairs). Position bed for access from both sides.
E	Ending	Disengages completely from daily decisions and work.	Remains in decision-making role and is fully responsible for day-to-day work.	Finds ways to support caregivers (e.g., sitting with dying person, delivering care package).	Remove equipment that is not needed. Do a sensory review.

Appendix B
(Examples of Important Tasks)

- Complete or update the advance directive and medical durable power of attorney for the dying person.
- Create or update a will/trust.
- Add or update the financial durable power of attorney or designated person to all accounts, insurance policies, and transfer on death (TOD) designations.
- Work with the dying person's doctor or hospice to determine how to handle medical emergencies that happen outside the hospital. Most states require a medical order signed by a physician, sometimes known as Physician Orders for Life-Sustaining Treatment or POLST.
- List the dying person's:

  - Bank and savings/checking account numbers
  - Retirement accounts
  - Life insurance policies
  - Credit cards
  - Mortgages or debts
  - Attorney and financial advisor
  - Valuable property

- Account names and passwords of online accounts, memberships, and subscriptions

- Combine or close financial accounts.
- Designate the person who will close out any online social media accounts (e.g., Facebook, Twitter, Instagram, Snapchat) after death.
- Collect important papers and information including but not limited to:

    - Birth certificates and citizenship, adoption, marriage, or divorce documents
    - Previous year's tax forms
    - Car titles
    - Original deed of trust for home and property
    - Safe deposit box and key

- Give the list of and the location of important documents to key people.
- Make decisions about funeral and burial or cremation. Finalize the arrangements.
- Give any instructions regarding obituary.
- Identify any people with whom you need to reconcile.

Additional resources:

Getting Your Affairs in Order

https://www.nia.nih.gov/health/getting-your-affairs-order

Eldercare Locator

https://eldercare.acl.gov/Public/Index.aspx

CaringInfo - National Hospice and Palliative Care Organization

http://www.caringinfo.org/i4a/pages/index.cfm?pageid=1

Appendix C (PACE Checklist)

Partnering Checklist

The Dying Person

❏ Review the stages of grieving and compare your experiences.

❏ Complete critical tasks (e.g., finance, legal and funeral planning). See Appendix B (Examples of Important Tasks).

❏ Talk and plan for who will take over daily work and provide them the needed information.

❏ Create and finish your bucket list.

❏ Be aware of changes in your physical abilities and adjust to them.

❏ Review your sense likes and dislikes and communicate them.

❏ Talk to your hospice team about your medications (which ones to stop, and how to manage pain and avoid constipation).

❏ Share what matters to you now and at the end of your life.

❏ Share your confidence with others that they will be fine after your death.

The Caregiver

- ❏ Identify how you can express your sadness in a way that is helpful to you.
- ❏ Identify circles of support. Consider how you might communicate with them.
- ❏ Identify who will be your caregiver.
- ❏ Learn about all the services offered by your hospice team.
- ❏ Be ready to tell people how they can help.
- ❏ Create a self-care plan.

The Family

- ❏ Plan your visit(s)--now and later.
- ❏ Become the caregiver's caregiver.

Environmental

- ❏ Discuss and decide where to spend this and each phase of the dying process and make plans accordingly.
- ❏ Assess trip hazards (e.g., throw rugs, transitions between carpet and flat surface, clutter on floor, oxygen tubing).
- ❏ Falls are common. Make a plan for what to do if a fall occurs.
- ❏ Are there changes that can be made now, especially to the bathroom (e.g., toilet seat riser, shower chair)?
- ❏ Talk to your hospice team about all environmental issues.

Assisting Checklist

The Dying Person

❏ Communicate your perspective for maintaining dignity, e.g., conserve dignity by:

- living in the moment,
- maintaining normalcy, and
- seeking spiritual comfort.

❏ Recognize what you can and can't do safely without help.

❏ Work with your healthcare team regarding tips for daily activities.

❏ Save energy and good days for completing your priorities.

❏ Add or increase water, foods high in fiber, and medications to promote regularity as you add or increase pain meds.

The Caregiver

❏ Be aware that the loss of independence can be difficult.

❏ Tell the dying person how you feel about them.

❏ Practice dignity-conserving practices like living in the moment and maintaining normalcy.

❏ Remind yourself: you are caring for someone you love when they need you the most.

❏ Pay attention to changes in the dying person and let the hospice team know if something seems wrong.

❏ Journal daily with observations and questions that come up.

❏ Prioritize self-care.

❏ Let others know your preference about communication regarding visits.

❏ Make sure you know how to assist the dying person safely. Ask the hospice team for guidance.

❏ Learn and use the many services available through hospice.

❏ Honor alone time.

❏ Assess how you are doing with the eight dimensions of wellness.

The Family

❏ Offer help. If it's not clear what's needed, let the caregiver know what you will help with and when you will help. Honor their wishes, if they say no.

❏ Caregiver's caregiver should start regular in-person check-ins.

❏ Make sure there aren't too many visitors. Look for the right balance.

❏ If there are unresolved issues, address them. The hospice team can help with this.

❑ Be involved. Your loved one is on their deathbed. Connect with them or their caregiver at any time in any way that is helpful.

Environmental

❑ Assess sleeping arrangements for both the dying person and caregiver.

❑ Do a sense review with Appendix E (The Senses).

❑ Determine if there are changes that can be made now, especially to the bathroom.

❑ Assess what equipment is needed.

❑ Talk to your hospice team about environmental issues.

Caring Checklist

The Dying Person
- ❏ Consider prioritizing safety over independence. Communicate your preferences.
- ❏ Work with your hospice team for tips to help with activities of daily living.
- ❏ Ask for and allow others to help.
- ❏ Communicate if you are in pain.

The Caregiver
- ❏ Objectively work through what it will take for you to provide care safely.
- ❏ Communicate any concerns about your ability to provide care at this level.
- ❏ Reach out for assistance to reserve your energy.
- ❏ Leave the bedside/house routinely.
- ❏ Communicate with your circles of support. Tell them what you need.
- ❏ Learn about respite care.
- ❏ Lean on your caregiver for support. Let them give you time for yourself.
- ❏ Talk to the hospice team if the dying patient says things that are hurtful to you or if you feel bad about saying hurtful things to the dying person.

❏ Talk to the hospice team if the dying person has uncharacteristic behavior (e.g., awake at night, sleeping during the day).

❏ Offer time alone with the dying person to others.

❏ Slow down. Explain what you are doing every time.

❏ Pace yourself. The Caring phase can last a long time.

❏ Re-assess environment for safety, especially for moving the dying person.

❏ Look for nonverbal signs of pain. Address pain early.

❏ Be proactive with both laxative and stool softeners for the dying person. Communicate to hospice team if either pain or constipation is not controlled.

The Family

❏ Check in with caregiver frequently regarding the level of care needed.

❏ Offer care for the caregiver.

❏ Practice supporting the caregiver's decisions, especially if you are not present daily.
Offer compliments, not suggestions. Ask permission if you must offer a suggestion.

❏ Give time for answers to form. Listen.

❏ Visit regularly, but adjust the time to their needs.

❏ If your role is changing, check in with the hospice team.

❏ Arrange for little luxuries. Focus care on comfort.

❏ Maintain the dying person's dignity. Provide privacy. Call before each visit.

❏ Continue to verbalize compassionate compliments in every direction.

Environmental

❏ Where is the best place for the dying person to be during this phase?

❏ How often is the dying person moving? Do you have enough pillows/wedges to allow for different, but comfortable, lying positions?

❏ Position the hospital bed so there is access from both sides. Raise the bed to waist level while providing care. Use a draw sheet and have two people provide care and movement in bed whenever possible. Lower the bed and raise guard rails after providing care.

❏ If the dying person attempts to get out of bed, tell your hospice team. Bed positioning and mats can minimize falls and injury.

❏ Do you have the right cleaning supplies?

❏ Look for trip hazards. Remove unneeded furniture. Add folding chairs for visitors.

❏ What is the view from the dying person's perspective?
❏ Think about what could reduce back strain on the caregiver.
❏ What equipment is needed?
❏ Do a sense review with the Appendix E (The Senses).

Ending Checklist

The Dying Person
- ❏ If the dying person previously asked for specific things before or at their death, now is the time to make them happen.

The Caregiver
- ❏ Consider sharing caregiver responsibility with others. Take shifts.

  For the dying person:
  - Partner with your hospice team to review what to expect and to have a plan.
  - Allow for food and drink to decrease and stop based on the dying person's cues.
  - Provide support and comfort with your presence.
  - Work with your hospice team on how to address swallowing issues.
  - Provide quiet support if the dying person sees or talks to someone who isn't there.
  - If the dying person says something hurtful, know this is normal and seek support.
  - If the dying person is short of breath, talk to your hospice team immediately.
  - Address pain based on the dying person's wishes and by what you observe.
  - Bathe and apply lotion as needed.

- Reposition the dying person but not at the expense of comfort.
- Place absorbent pads under the dying person.
- Hold hands or place your hand on the dying person's chest where blood flow concentrates between the heart and brain.
- Talk to the dying person, not about them, even after death.

For the Caregiver, Family, and Friends:
- Consider sharing caregiver responsibility with others. Take shifts.
- Communicate to their circles of support.
- Use respite care as needed without guilt.
- Create an environment that is supportive of both the dying person and you.
- Set limits for visitors that meet your needs.
- Offer alone time for family and friends.
- Follow the dying person's wishes but do not harm yourself in the process.
- Know that it is normal and okay to hope death will occur soon.
- Embrace hugs if they bring you comfort.

The Family

❏ If you can, become a caregiver, but keep the primary caregiver in their role.

❏ If you cannot become a caregiver, support the caregiver(s) in their role.

❏ Support the caregiver. Tell them that they are doing a good job—repeatedly.

❏ Offer practical support unless it's turned down (e.g., cleaning up the house, doing laundry).

❏ Show physical affection with hugs if it brings comfort and is culturally acceptable.

❏ Tell the dying person what you want them to know. It's never too late.

❏ Read, talk, or sing to the dying person.

❏ Ask for alone time with the dying person if desired.

❏ Bring a comforting gift for the caregiver.

Environmental

❏ Create a comfortable environment.

❏ Have healthy drinks and snacks available for those taking shifts.

❏ Equipment that was useful a week ago is no longer needed. Move it out of the room and out of your way.

❏ Do a sense review with the Appendix E (The Senses).

After Death Checklist
- ❏ Take a few minutes with the person after their death to fully experience the moment.
- ❏ Call your hospice team. They will contact the coroner and funeral home.
- ❏ Call family members.
- ❏ If you are comfortable, prepare or assist the hospice worker in preparing the body.
- ❏ Dispose of medications properly.
- ❏ Keep bereavement support information nearby and use it for you and your family.

Appendix D
(Activities of Daily Living [ADLs])

Activities of Daily Living, or ADLs, is a nursing term that defines a set of activities necessary for daily self-care. The specific activities monitored and addressed by medical personnel are: walking (loco-motion), transferring or movement from one place to another, movement in bed, transfers, dressing, feeding, and personal hygiene.

Moving Around (Locomotion)

Includes: walking on a flat, level floor, on gentle slopes, and down stairs. During any phase, the dying person may need a cane, walker, or wheelchair to get around. Usually, if someone must have support from another person or leans on things when they move around (sometimes called a "furniture walker") it is time to start using something to help. The hospice team can figure out if a cane or walker might help and provide instruction on how to use and adjust them. Three key tips: 1) Create a clear (not cluttered), well-lighted path around the house or room, 2) slow down and don't make quick turns, and 3) avoid carrying an armload of things that can block your view or change your balance while walking.

Consider:

- There are many choices to moving around as safely as possible. Here are some general points to consider.

    - Canes come with many different shaped handles for style and comfort. Walking sticks can be helpful for people who don't want to use a cane. Rubber tips or four-pronged bottoms provide additional stability. If the cane is adjustable, make sure the top of the cane is at the same height of the wrist when standing, and arms are relaxed at your side.
    - Walkers are available in many different styles. The height should be adjusted so the handles are at the height of the palm when standing, and arms are relaxed at your side.
    - Wheelchairs can make life easier. As soon as the wheelchair stops, it's important to lock the wheels. Be sure never to get a person in or out of the wheelchair without the wheels being locked.
    - Transport chairs are smaller than wheelchairs. The wheels are easier to maneuver if a person uses their feet to move around while sitting in the chair.

- Chairs with arms make it easier to stand. The arms provide a place to hold on to.

Transferring or Moving From One Place to Another

Includes: After the dying person is no longer able to walk or stand on their own, they will need the caregiver to help move them from one place to another. This can include moving from bed to chair, sitting to standing, or on and off the bedside commode or bed.

Consider:

1. The bed. An adjustable bed is safer because it can be lowered to a height where the person's feet are flat on the floor. If a bed is too high, the person may slide off to reach the floor creating a chance of falling. If the bed is too low (hips are lower than their knees), they will have difficulty getting out of the bed.

2. There are four general phases to getting out of a bed:

   a. Start with sitting up in bed.
   b. Sit on the side of the bed with feet flat on the floor.
   c. Stand by the side of bed. Before walking, shift weight from left to right foot.
   d. Begin walking slowly.

3. Gait belt: This is a strap that wraps around the dying person's waist to give the caregiver something to hold onto when helping them move from one place to another. The dying person wears the belt and must be able to bear most of their own weight. To use a gait belt safely, the dying person should only need a small nudge to stabilize and balance. Gait belts can range in price from $8 to $25 depending on the style. Hospice may provide them as part of their service.

4. If the dying person is physically weak/unstable or mentally confused or combative, consider using more than one person during the transfers.

5. Lifting a weight of more than 35 pounds and below your knees is putting you at risk of injury. Once the dying person is not able to get themselves off the floor with minimal assistance, every option that minimizes their time out of the bed should be considered.

6. With use of a sling, a mechanical lift can safely move someone who is unable to bear any weight at all. Many models and features are available based on physical ability of the person being moved and the environment space where the maneuvers are required. These lifts can range between $1,200 - $6,000,

so they may not be an option for many people. It is more affordable for people with prolonged incapacity. Hospice may provide a lift.

Movement in Bed

Includes: sitting up, moving around in the bed, scooting up toward the head of the bed, and getting out of the bed.

Consider:
- Before moving a person in a bed, raise the bed to the caregiver's hips to minimize strain on the back.
- A 3-foot x 3-foot cloth pad (or a flat sheet folded in thirds) placed under the buttocks and lower back of a person in bed can be grasped by two people on either side of the bed to move the person up in the bed safely. Move with a count of three: one, two, three, move. Using a pad prevents injury to the person's skin by reducing friction between the skin and sheet and helps to avoid "road rash/carpet burn." It is also more comfortable than being hoisted from under the arms. If the person is in a hospital bed, lower the head of the bed flat before the move to make the slide easier. Raise the foot of the bed. Always raise the bed so those doing the

lifting don't have to bend over and return it to a safe level afterward.
- Placing a large plastic trash bag between the pad and the bed will reduce friction and make moving the person up in bed easier. Note: Remove the bag after moving them up in bed or they will slip back down!
- A trapeze attached to the bed allows a person with arm strength to maneuver in bed.

Dressing

Includes: putting on socks, stockings, and shoes, as well as clothing, e.g., shirt and pants.

Consider:
- Dressing aids and devices that can be helpful include sock assist tools, long-handled shoe horns, button hooks, and zipper pulls. All are available to buy on the Internet. Many are available at local drug stores.
- Pants with elastic or drawstrings are easier.
- Slip-on shoes are helpful.
- Adapt T-shirts to open in the back and close with Velcro®. These shirts are also available on the Internet. Use key words like adaptive, Velcro®, back opening, and shirt in your search. You can also cut a shirt in back up

to the neck and tuck it gently behind the person if they are bed bound.

Eating or Feeding

Includes: the process of drinking or eating.

Consider:
- Cutting food into smaller pieces.
- A hospital bed or pillows so the person can sit up while eating, reducing the risk of choking.
- Bendable straws and cups with lids to reduce spilling.
- Spoons with a larger grip and soft, rubbery edges.
- Thickeners to make swallowing liquids easier.
- A blender to purée foods when swallowing becomes an issue. There are recipes on the Internet. Applesauce and pudding can be bought in individual servings.

Personal Hygiene or Bathing

Includes: grooming, and washing of face, body, arms, feet, legs, and between legs.

Consider:

- Tools like long-handled combs are helpful for reaching the back of the head.
- A straight bench in the shower provides stability and comfort.
- An extension shower head that is in reach and will direct water where needed.
- Bathmats that provide a consistent texture and that can be cleaned are the most safe.
- Grab bars in the shower are ideal. There are temporary ones that use suction and can be moved or removed easily.
- Some personal hygiene can be done by professionals. When people ask, "What can I do to help?" suggest that they arrange for a hairstylist or a professional manicurist or pedicurist to come to the home. To assist those with diabetes, someone specially trained will be needed to prevent injury or infection.

Toileting

Includes: peeing or urinating (also called "voiding" or "output" by medical professionals) and pooping (also called "bowel movement", "BM," or "defecation").

Consider: Toileting equipment needs will change as the person becomes weaker. Some types include, usually in this order:

- Toilet frame (It looks like a walker and is placed directly on top of toilet. The frame provides arms to help with sitting and standing.)
- Bedside commode
- Bedpans
- Absorbing pads to place on bed (3 foot x 3 foot). Also useful for repositioning in bed.
- Absorbent underwear or adult diapers
- Catheter (This is a flexible tube that is placed into the urethra that collects urine automatically. This eliminates the need to get out of bed—no mess. The bag must be emptied regularly, and infection prevention techniques must be followed.)

Handy cleaning supplies for the caregiver:

- Keep a box of gloves (latex free) nearby.
- Have hand sanitizer in every room.
- Use dark towels especially if there is any bleeding or diarrhea.
- Set washing machine to hot when washing to kill germs.
- Develop a system to get dirty towels out of the room and washed quickly to minimize odor.

Appendix E (The Senses)

As people die, their senses change. Revisit this table often as a reference. Note that there may be differences in preference between the dying person and caregiver. Consider both people. During the Ending phase, the dying person may care less about their senses than the caregiver does.

The Senses

	Partnering	Assisting
Sight	-take walks/drives -look at old photos -videotape favorite places for later	-decorate with things you both want to see -provide a view out the window
Hearing	-list your favorite songs/artists -try new routines, e.g., music hour	-move noisy equipment like Oxygen to another room -experiment with radio stations
Touch	-many hospices offer therapeutic massages -hug more	-ask permission before touching -offer hand holding, back & foot rubs and notice response
Taste	-enjoy favorite foods -going forward, food may not taste as it did before	-appetite can change daily -serve small portions -focus on favorite, comfort foods
Smell	-smells can be pleasant or nauseating -observe preferences	-create a system for timely disposal or washing of soiled items -don't wear perfume

Caring	Ending
-adjust lighting and view for the dying person -keep a reading light & glasses by the bedside	-use a lamp for softer lighting
-avoid constant TV -try soft music or a fan for white noise -baby monitors can be helpful for caregivers peace of mind	-ask visitors to share their favorite music -consider playing generic music if preferences are unknown
-say it before you do it, e.g., "I'm going to lift your arm." -loosen sheets around feet -moisturize dry skin	-encourage physical contact with the dying person - focus on the upper chest and head
-it is normal for appetite to change -offer food but do not force it -look for other ways to give comfort	-appetite decreases and stops -caregivers and visitors benefit from healthy drinks and snacks
-smells of bodily fluids affect everyone -open a window and use a fan to dissipate odors	-consider essential oils or incense, if tolerated

References

Amelia Goranson, Ryan Ritter, Adam Waytz, Michael I. Norton, and Kurt Gray (2017) ,"Losing Our Most Special Possession: the Unexpected Positivity of Dying", in NA - Advances in Consumer Research Volume 45, eds. Ayelet Gneezy, Vladas Griskevicius, and Patti Williams, Duluth, MN : Association for Consumer Research, Pages: 228-232. http://www.acrwebsite.org/volumes/1024719/volumes/v45/NA-45

Angela Morrow, RN | Reviewed by Richard N. Fogoros, MD. (n.d.). How to Recognize When Your Loved One Is Dying. Retrieved November 17, 2017, from https://www.verywell.com/the-journey-towards-death-1132504

Care of the Body After Death (n.d.). Retrieved November 20, 2017, from http://www.virtualhospice.ca/en_US/Main+Site+Navigation/Home/Topics/Topics/Final+-Days/Care+of+the+Body+After+Death.aspx

Center for Drug Evaluation and Research. (n.d.). Safe Disposal of Medicines - Disposal of Unused Medicines: What You Should Know. Retrieved from https://www.fda.gov/Drugs/ResourcesForYou/Consumers/BuyingUs-ingMedicineSafely/EnsuringSafeUseofMedicine/SafeDis-posalofMedicines/ucm186187.htm

Chapter 16 Activities of Daily Living - Veteran's Review Board, 219 Chapter 16 Activities of Daily Living INTRO-

DUCTION The Activities of Daily Living (ADLs) are a defined set of activities necessary for normal self-care. http://www.vrb.gov.au/pubs/garp-chapter16.pdf

Chochinov, H. M. (2002). Dignity-conserving care--a new model for palliative care: helping the patient feel valued. *JAMA, 287*(17), 2253–2260.

Coping with Loss: Bereavement and Grief. (2015, May 01). Retrieved November 20, 2017, from http://www.mental-healthamerica.net/conditions/coping-loss-bereavement-and-grief

End of Life : Helping with Comfort and Care. (July 2016 NIH Publication No. 16-6036). Retrieved November 17, 2017, from https://order.nia.nih.gov/sites/default/files/2017-07/End_of_Life_508.pdf

Frechen, S., Zoeller, A., Ruberg, K., Voltz, R., & Gaertner, J. (2012). Drug Interactions in Dying Patients. *Drug Safety, 35*(9), 745-758. doi:10.1007/bf03261971

Head, B., Ritchie, C. S., & Smoot, T. M. (2005). Prognostication in Hospice Care: Can the Palliative Performance Scale Help? *Journal of Palliative Medicine, 8*(3), 492-502. doi:10.1089/jpm.2005.8.492

If you can't do it, adapt it! (n.d.). Retrieved November 20, 2017, from http://www.adaptiveequipmentcorner.com/

Institute for Healthcare Improvement, Person- and Family-Centered Care - IHI Home Page. (n.d.). Retrieved November 17, 2017, from http://www.ihi.org/topics/PFCC/Pages/default.aspx

Mclean, S., Sheehy-Skeffington, B., O'Leary, N., & O'Gorman, A. (2012). Pharmacological management of co-morbid conditions at the end of life: is less more? *Irish Journal of Medical Science, 182*(1), 107-112. doi:10.1007/s11845-012-0841-6

New on Canadian Virtual Hospice. (n.d.). Retrieved November 17, 2017, from http://www.virtualhospice.ca/en_US/Main Site Navigation/Home.aspx

On Death and Dying (n.d.) Elisabeth Kubler-Ross, Retrieved November 18, 2017, from http://www.ekrfoundation.org/five-stages-of-grief/

Radcliff, D. N. (2017, May 01). How to deal with death, loss, grief, bereavement. Retrieved November 20, 2017, from https://www.washingtontimes.com/news/2017/may/1/health-how-deal-death-loss-grief-bereavement/

Eight Dimensions of Wellness. Retrieved from https://www.samhsa.gov/wellness-initiative/eight-dimensions-wellness

When Is It Safe to Manually Lift a Patient? *AJN, American Journal of Nursing,107*(8), 59. doi:10.1097/01.naj.0000282297.26312.d8 http://www.asphp.org/wp-content/uploads/2011/05/When_Is_It_Safe_To_Manually_Lift_A_Patient.pdf

When Death is Near, Canadian Virtual Hospice. (n.d.). Retrieved November 17, 2017, from http://www.virtualhospice.ca/en_US/Main+Site+Navigation/Home/Topics/Topics/Final+Days/When+Death+is+Near.aspx

About the Authors

Kim Gladstone, RN, CHPN, MA has more than 30 years of experience in healthcare spanning diverse areas in both direct care and as an administrator. In each role, she worked to understand best practices and then shared what she learned with providers and patients to improve communication and standardization with the ultimate goal of improving care. She is currently practicing as a hospice nurse in St. Louis, Missouri.

Laurie Wolf, PhD., CPE, ASQ-CSSBB is a Certified Professional Ergonomist with a PhD in Human Factors & Ergonomics from Loughborough University in the United Kingdom. She is a Certified Six Sigma Black Belt from the American Society of Quality. She has over 25 years of experience in the healthcare environment and has published more than 20 peer-reviewed articles and 4 book chapters. Her focus is on quality improvement projects to achieve efficient processes and error proofing that result in a safe environment for staff and patients.

Made in the USA
Columbia, SC
20 January 2021